Muse Mantra
Colouring Meditations

to calm your mind and soothe your soul

Julia Harvey

The right of Julia Harvey to be identified as the author of this work has been asserted in accordance with the Copyright, Designs and Patents Act 1988.

© Julia Harvey 2018

All rights reserved. No part of this publication may be reproduced, stored in a retrieval system, or transmitted at any time or by any means, electronic, mechanical, photocopying, recording or otherwise without the prior permission of the copyright holder.

ISBN-10: 1544957971
ISBN-13: 9781544957975

Published by Julia Harvey Designs www.juliaharveydesigns.co.uk

Printed by CreateSpace, An Amazon.com Company.

DEDICATION

William, Luna and Honey

Lucy and Pudding

ACKNOWLEDGMENTS

This book is dedicated to the women in this book from around the world. They were brave and courageous, stepping up for me to draw them, giving me the honour of capturing their Inner Muse.

Thank you, Joy Sisters.

Adriane, Alia, Amanda, Amy B, Amy H, Amy W, Angela, Angelina, Angie, Ann, Barbara, Brandi, Brandy, Cassia, Cathy, Cheryn, Chessa, Chrissy, Christina, Christine, Christy, Cristen, Debbi, Eithne, Emily, Erin, Fay, Gwynn, Hannah, Heather, Izabela, Jana, Jeannine, Jennifer B, Jennifer G, Jenny, Jessica, Jill, Julia Mc, Julia (me) Kari, Kate, Kelly, Kyra, Leah, Linda, Lisa, Liz, Loran, Lori, Lyn, Malika, Marnie, Mary, Melissa E, Melissa M, Melissa S, Nadine, Nancy, Paula, Peg, Persephone, Rachel, Renee, Ruth, Samantha, Sarah R, Sarah W, Sarah G, Sheena, Sheila, Stacy, Tara, Tracye, Vanessa S, Vanessa W.

To Hannah Marcotti for facilitating the online group programme Holiday Joy where this project was born.

Mistifonts www.mistifonts.com for the colouring font to accompany the Muse.

| SECTIONS

Foreword by Hannah Marcotti

1| About Muse Mantras

2| Colouring as Meditation

3| Colouring Hints

4| Space to try out your colourful supplies

5| Once Upon A Time

6| The 76 Muse Mantra Colouring Pages

7| About Julia Harvey

FOREWORD

I was 35, nursing a baby while typing words that would become my first blog post. I wrote about a meal I had made. The post was 2 paragraphs long. Those two paragraphs took me hours to craft. The feeling that rushed through me as I hit publish was fear mixed with this tingle of delight. That tingle is what I would come to discover was being held by my Joy.

Joy is not a momentary feeling, it is an emotion that holds all other emotions inside of it. When you are in the place of deep sadness that turns to laughter through the tears, Joy is wrapping her arms around you. The deeper we feel, feel all of it, the more we open to the bubble of Joy.

All those years ago with my third baby on my hip I noticed that the thing we all seemed to be collectively searching for was a deeper Joy in our lives. Joy as the container for living in deep truth, intense beauty, sacred purpose, devoted bodies, intimate love.

I wondered if I could gather 100 women to collectively raise our vibration of Joy together in circle, and that wonder became The Joy Up. The Joy Up lived for years becoming and becoming with the women who had said YES to claiming deeper Joy. The Joy Up became a community of stories, projects, choice and change. It became bigger than what I had created with an idea, it was now pulsing with the ideas of hundreds of women.

I remember the day an envelope came in the mail and I saw myself looking back at me, the self through Julia's eyes. She was so elegant and there was a twinkle in her eyes. The Joy Up circle would become filled with these drawings. I would watch women seeing themselves through Julia's art, seeing themselves with softness and tenderness, perhaps for the first time. To hold in your hands, your beauty, your wonder, your gifts, your uniqueness, this is truly being seen.

Joy isn't something we feel in short bursts, Joy is a temple of devotion to this amazing life.

Thank you Julia, for showing so many of us who we were when we needed help seeing it. Thank you for being part of the movement of joy so many years ago. Thank you for blessing us with this collection of Joy.

1 | MUSE MANTRAS

Muse Mantras are spirit-lifting, soul-soothing, mindful art with Reiki channelled within each illustration. Reiki is a Japanese word, meaning Universal Life Energy (Rei- universal life, Ki – energy.)

Every Muse begins with an original illustration, drawn by hand, with pencils, pens and professional markers, adding a Mantra to complete. A Mantra, used within the Hindu and Buddhist traditions is a word, sound or phrase repeated over and over, to aid concentration in meditation. Usually written in Sanskrit, I was inspired in my own meditation practice to design these innovative pieces with an English mantra, a statement or positive affirmation that could support emotional wellness.

Whilst drawing, I am sharing Reiki and weaving Reiki symbols into the sketch, there are three I use, the first for mental and emotional well-being; the second, for healing past hurts and the third, balancing any present issues.

Because of the Reiki placed within, when you spend time with a Muse Mantra, you are experiencing 'soothing vibrations.'

All the Muse Mantras in this book can be used as powerful totems and talismans in your day-to-day life, in meditation spaces, on altars, shelves, as prompts for writing in your journal, placed on vision boards, stuck in visual books, even as bookmarks.

Over the years, I began to feel that Muse Mantras would make a wonderful colouring book for adults and this is how Muse Mantra Colouring Meditations was born.

The 76 women featured in this colouring compendium have a very special story to be told.

It was holiday season, 2012, I was finishing up a commission of drawing wedding guests, whilst also taking part in Holiday Joy, an online programme run by Hannah Marcotti in USA. In this group gathered a tribe of women from all over the world. As a holiday gift to them, I asked if anyone would like me to draw them, thinking that a handful would step forward. I was taken aback at 20, 40, 60, 70+ coming forward! Wow this was amazing.

Over the next few months, I began to illustrate each woman who had tentatively raised her hand, sharing the finished portrait in the private Facebook group. What began as whimsical and fun turned into a magical process, I was capturing the essence of each woman and we were all witnessing seeing each in a very innovative way.

Over time, these initial drawings have been a catalyst for my own illustration and design work, giving me confidence to carry on drawing and to take myself seriously as an artist and illustrator. I knew that one day I would create something from this extra special project that was very dear to my heart.

Fast forward to 2017, I recognised that this project would make a wonderful colouring compendium and I set about contacting all of the women to find out if they had a specific mantra they would like me to include. I wasn't able to track everyone down, as some had left Facebook and I had no way of contacting them, but in the most part what you're experiencing right now, are real woman from all over the world sharing their mantra with you. Some let me choose, but for the most part, the mantra is theirs. Synchronistically, there were very few duplications.

I am proud to have birthed this book, I hope that you enjoy playing.

Julia xx

2 | COLOURING AS MEDITATION

In bringing together Muse Mantra Colouring Meditations, my aim is for you to use the colouring experience to create a calm moment in your daily life. We are all looking for a way to feel calm and peaceful and colouring is a great way to switch off. Whilst usually an activity reserved for children, it is proven that colouring can help alleviate tension and stress in adults.

Colouring can help you practice mindfulness, recommended as a way to train the brain away from focusing on every day worries.

It allows you to get absorbed in the moment and go back to a slower pace, where you can seek silence in the art of colouring.

This book is a long time coming. I used to turn to colouring as a child – it was my go-to activity to calm my mind as a young girl, never would I be seen without a colouring book by my bedside. Whilst dealing with a health problem in my 20s, it became a stress release. Now, it is something I have in my rebalancing toolkit.

Over the past 6 years, I have drawn around 350 Muse Mantra Portraits and will often hand out colouring pages for participants in workshops, with private clients, work colleagues, as well as friends and family.

The beginning phase of black lines and white space, a table with coloured pencils, a pot of felts and gel pens accompanied with a powerful positive mantra can really soothe your soul.

You're giving your whole self a colourful massage.

It seemed a natural transition to create a colouring compendium for calm.

3 | COLOURING HINTS

For this book, you can use professional markers, felt tip pens, or coloured pencils. If you choose Promarkers or felts, I would suggest slipping a sheet of copy paper or bleed proof paper in between the pages to protect the design on the next page. Cutting it to size and keeping it within the book will ensure you're always ready for colouring.

If you haven't tried professional markers, why not start with a set of skin tones. Some brands to consider would be Windsor and Newton, Letraset, Copic Ciao, all are alcohol markers so will blend over each other. You can use regular felt tips, but they won't blend and will be streaky for the face and skin but will be fine for the clothes and embellishments. If using these, three favourites are Berol, Paper Mate Flair and Staedtler. Wax pencils are a great addition too and can be used as a layer over markers, Prismacolour are pretty lovely. I would stay clear of watercolour paints or watercolour pencils on this particular paper as it won't fair very well when wet and avoid Sharpies.

You can also embellish the drawing, add extra layers, scarves, jewellery, glasses or tattoos.

To add to your colouring kit, pick up some gel pens, plain and sparkly, a Uni-Ball Signo Pen in white, gold and silver, Uni-Ball Black Fine Liner in 0.3 or 0.5. All these extra pens can add touches to your foundation coloured layer. Use hearts, stars, dots, dashes, flower leaves, petals, circles, lines, triangles etc. to add depth and character.

Having said all of this, colouring in is a process of letting go, so you can choose to scribble all over with chubby waxy crayons, if you'd like, release any tension and just feel free.

This is just guidance, there are no rules!

Colouring can also help you to journal

The process of colouring and journalling gives your conscious mind a break.

I have purposefully left clear space around the Muse Mantra, this can be used to note down any messages you receive whilst colouring. You may find a new phrase pops into your mind, or your unconscious thoughts are solving a problem and suddenly you are seeing things clearly. Use this space around the main image for writing notes, doodling and processing feelings. Remember to breathe smoothly and slowly - in through your nose and out through your nose, gently, calmly and with no hurry.

Keep the book handy, in your bag, with a small stash of supplies. Take it with you if you're going somewhere that makes you feel anxious, know that it's with you and you can flip through the book and turn to the Muse Mantra that can supportively calm and soothe you in that moment.

Guidance on how to use the book

Close your eyes and like an oracle deck, flip through the book and see where the page lands.

This Muse Mantra is calling you.

You can choose to use music as an accompaniment or savour the silence. If you're feeling stressed out and anxious, turn to a Muse Mantra Colouring Meditation to calm your mind and soothe your soul, so that when you have finished you return to the task at hand, feeling relaxed and centred.

4| SPACE TO TRY OUT YOUR COLOURFUL SUPPLIES

5 | ONCE UPON A TIME

Once upon a time,
women gathered around a virtual table
Slowly easing themselves into the festive season,
with Grace, Joy and Fairy Lights
Vision Books, Journalling and Dreams.

One by one
each woman bravely stepped forward,
to be drawn.
What began as whimsical and fun,
transformed into a deep longing.

They were being seen
by other women,
in a t-o-t-a-l-l-y new way.
They were seeing themselves, with kindness
and they discovered they were looking their Divine Self
in the eyes.

They felt soothed
sensual
and desired.

Each portrait
brought a shift.
Each woman saw
their beauty and light

and it reminded them
to be their own best friend

Starting with love
No judgments
Just honouring
their inner sparkle,
loving themselves
a little bit more.

The healing visual
was a gentle reminder
To nurture soul, spirit, body, mind
To calm
To soothe
and fall in love with their lives
their spaces, connections and purpose
To connect with their inner muse

They nudge you forward
To Dream
To Step into
your own light
Reconnect with who you are
Be that beautiful self
For, she's calling you

THE 76 MUSE MANTRA COLOURING PAGES

Start by doing one thing

The sight of the stars makes me dream

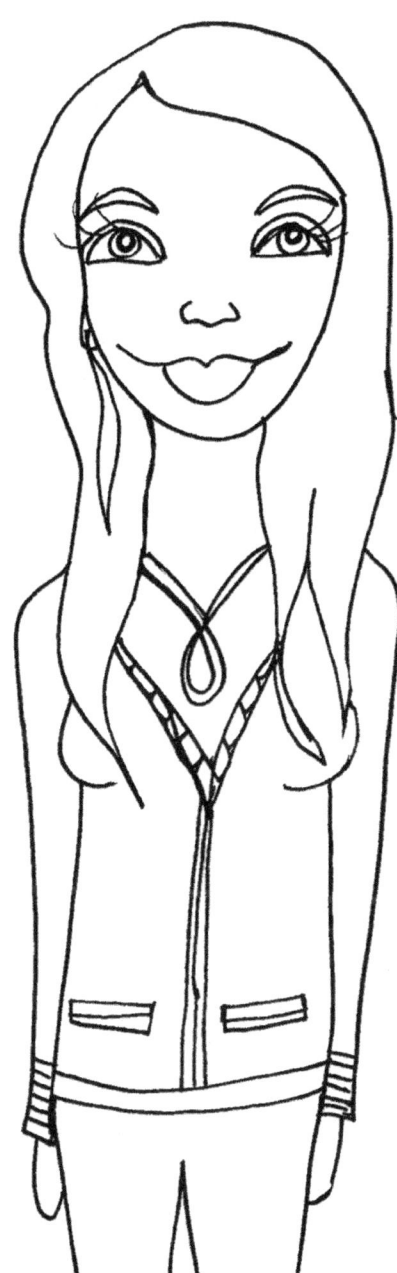

I am grateful

Simply
- Me -
Wild
and
Free

I am too blessed to stress

Let

go

All that I seek is already within me

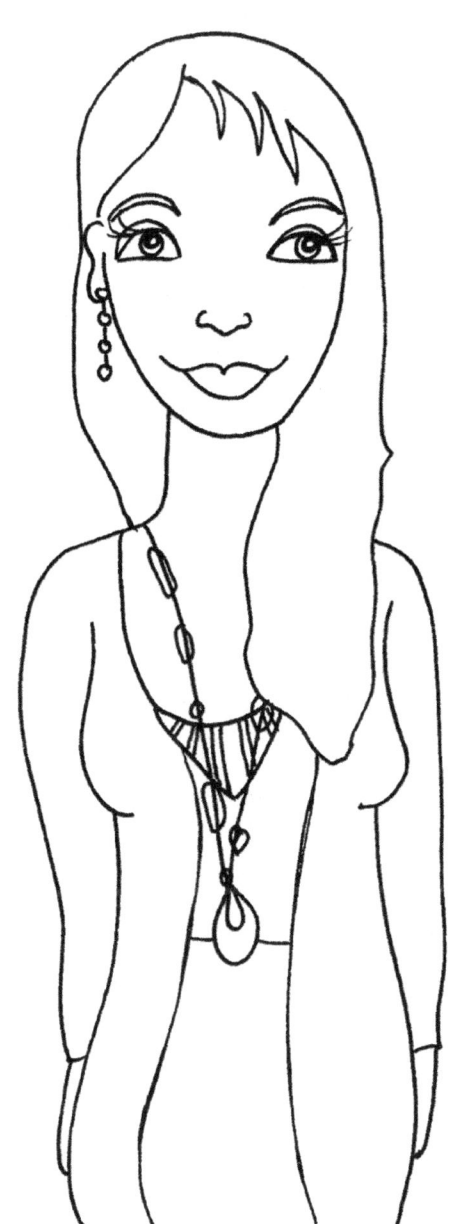

I inspire

I am stronger than I realise

I have a song to sing

Lose Your Fear

It is what it is

I see the world with beauty

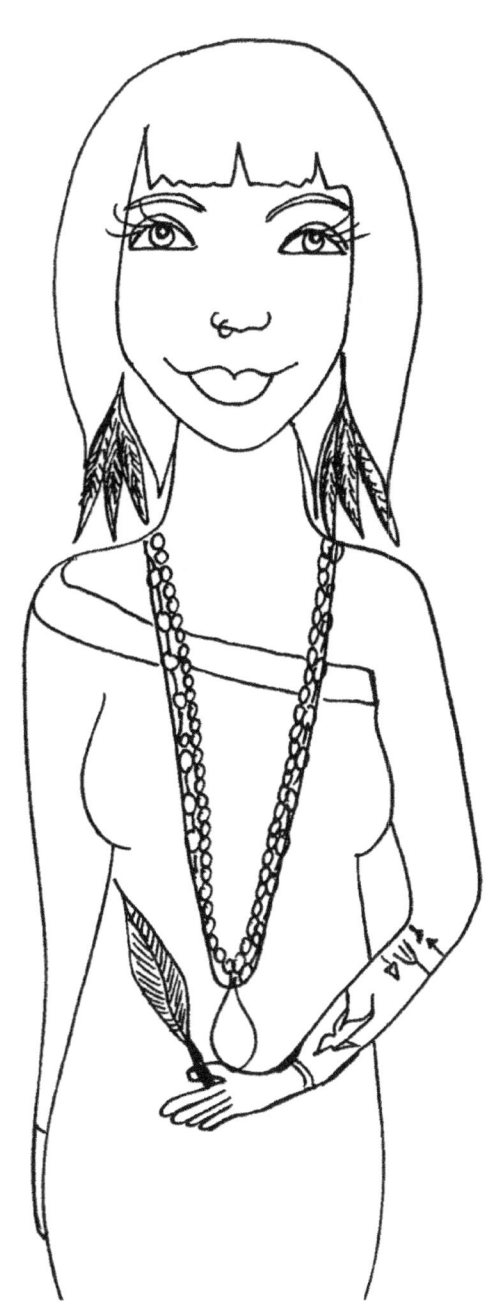

What Lights me up?

Be
Yourself

Dream

Evolve

As I look after myself my health begins to rebalance

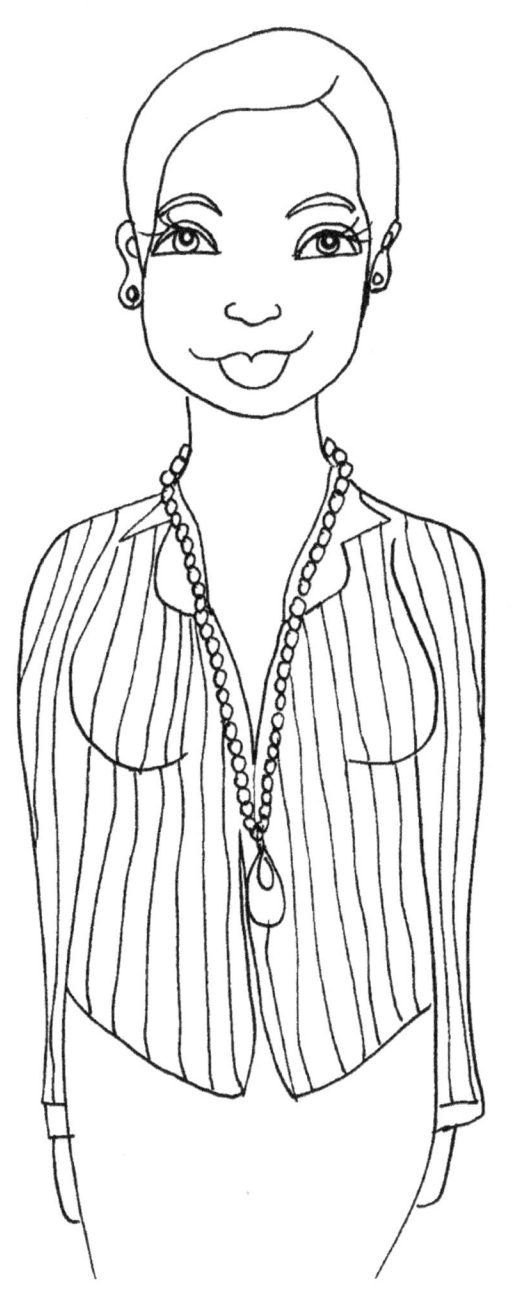

I am blessed

I love myself just the way I am

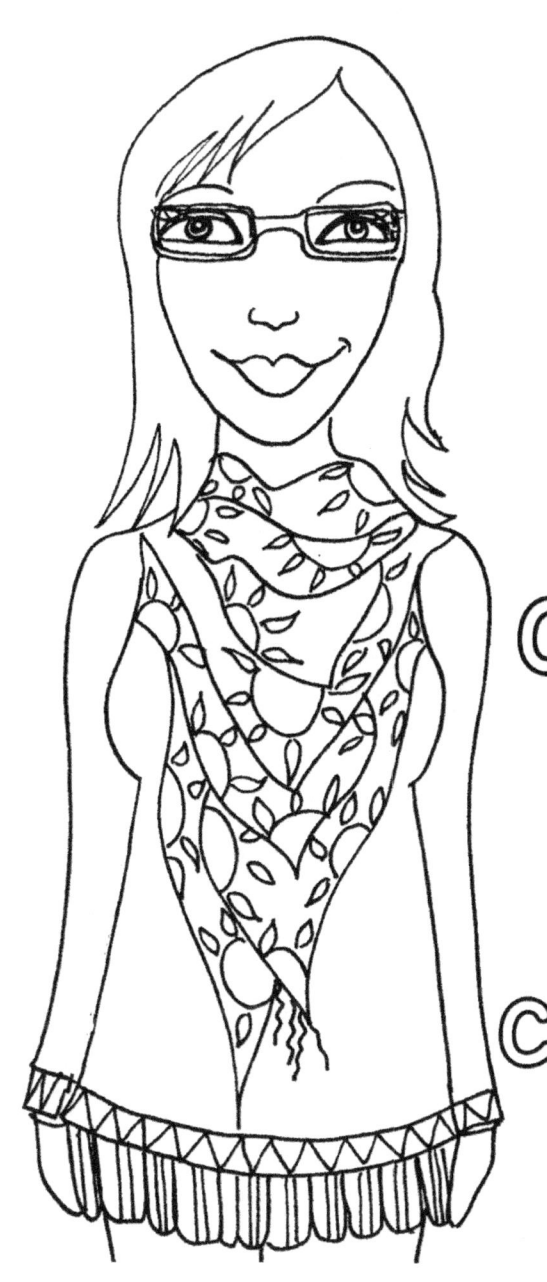

I am safe, I am loved, I am protected

I am rooted in wonder

I am a unique gift to the world

Find magic in the moments

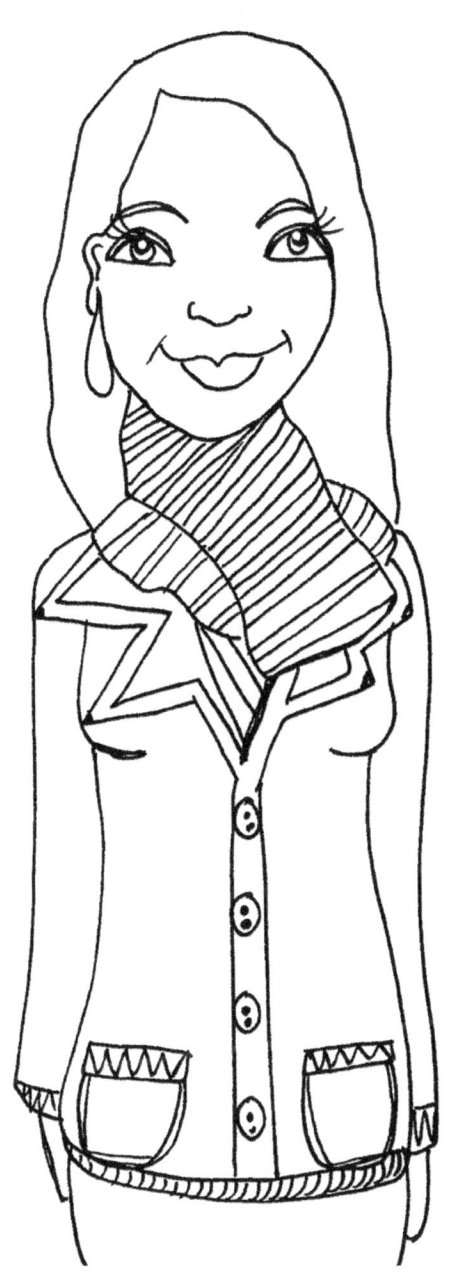

My intuition leads me towards brilliant, radiant possibilities

Making with your hand and feeling with your heart is where the true magic resides

Be kinder to your self

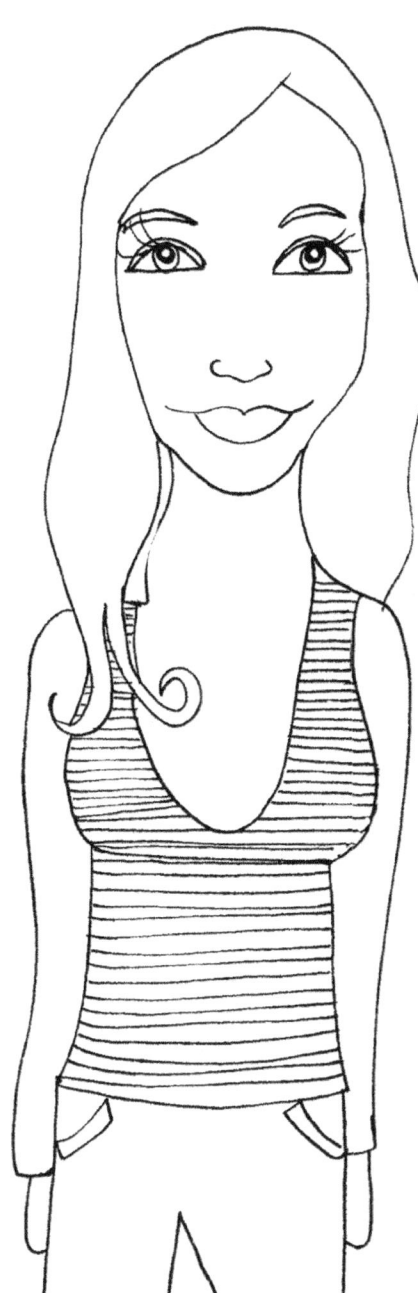

I value and accept myself

I have all the time I need

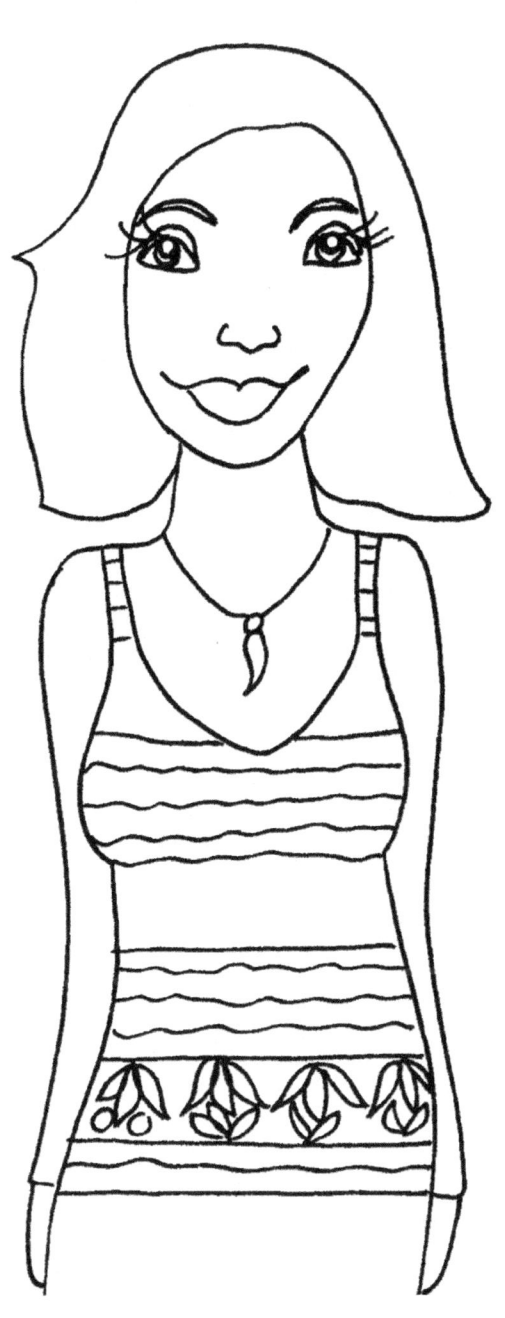

Kindness Matters

Blessings:
May I see them
May I be them

Focus on the good stuff

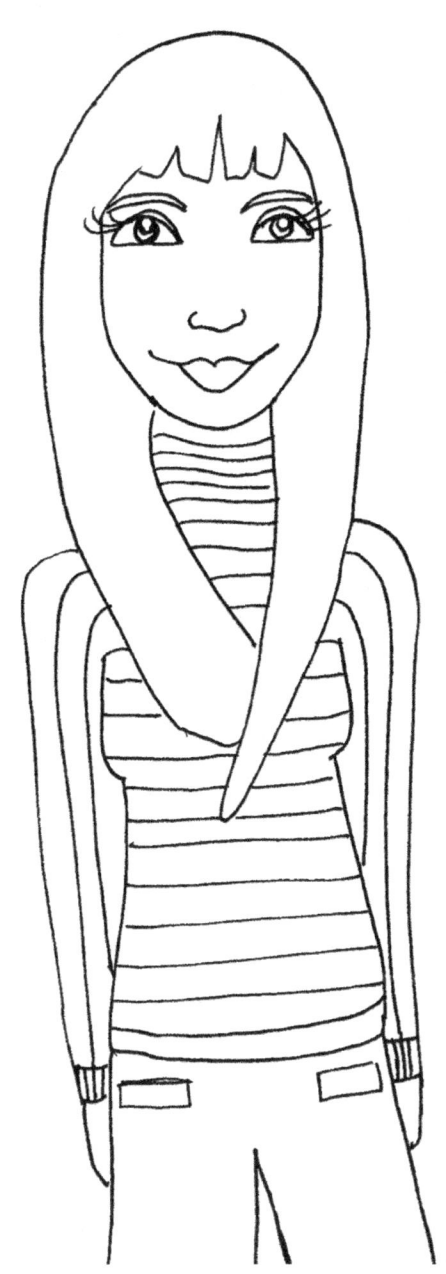

I am worthy of receiving abundance

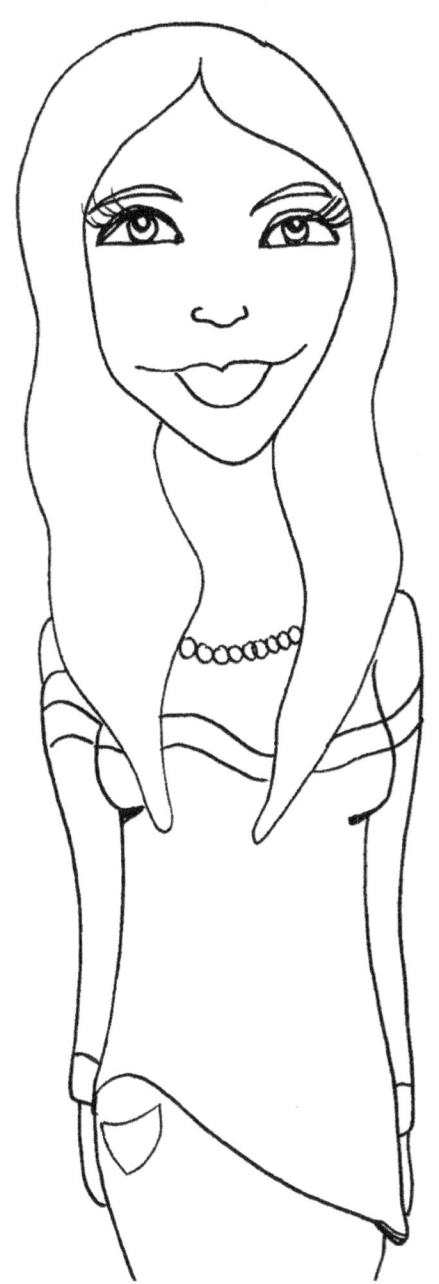

There is a State of Grace within me

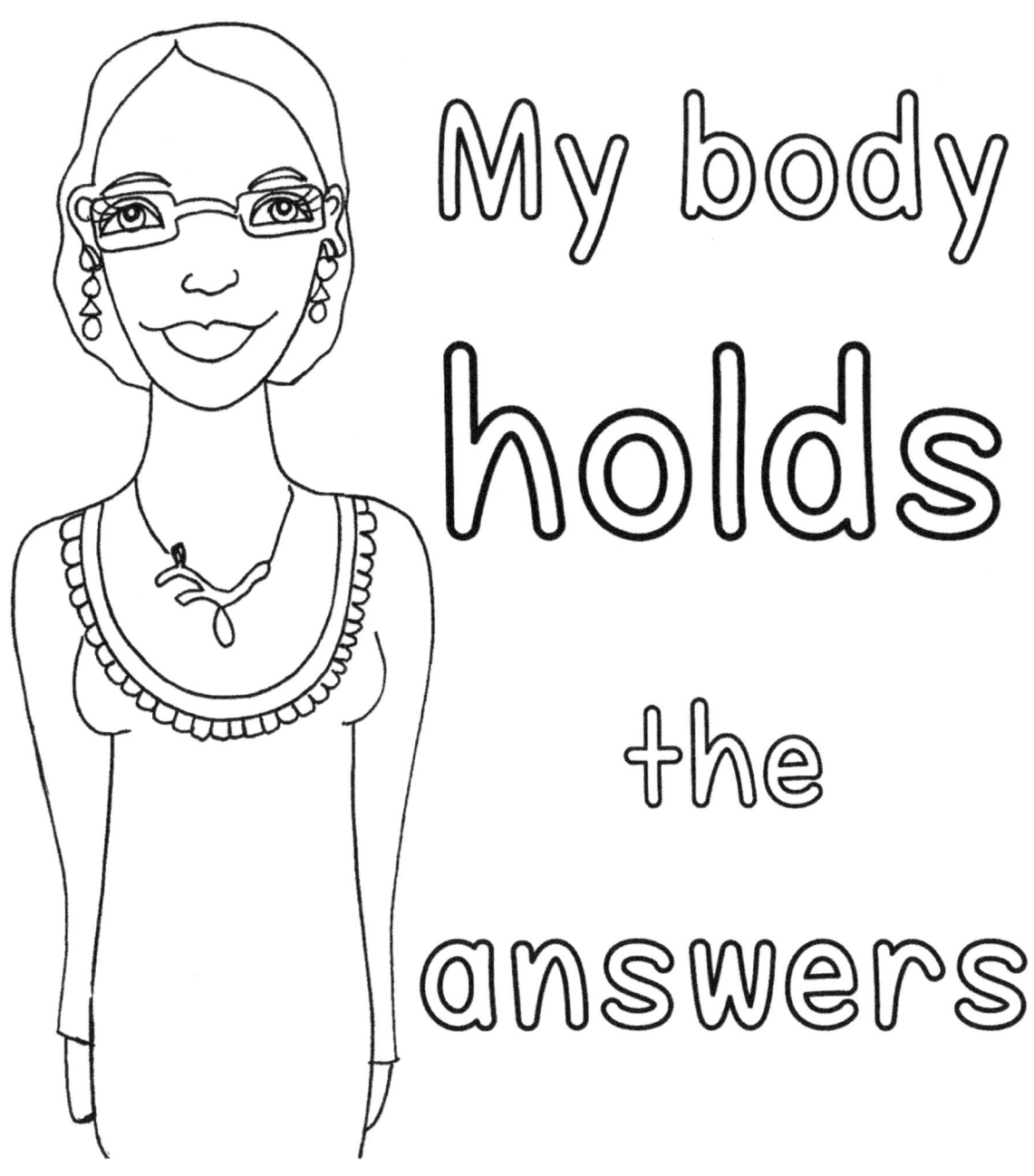

Transcend

Look

inward

Shine, in the warm glow of delight

You are a Deep Well

I live with intention and thrive

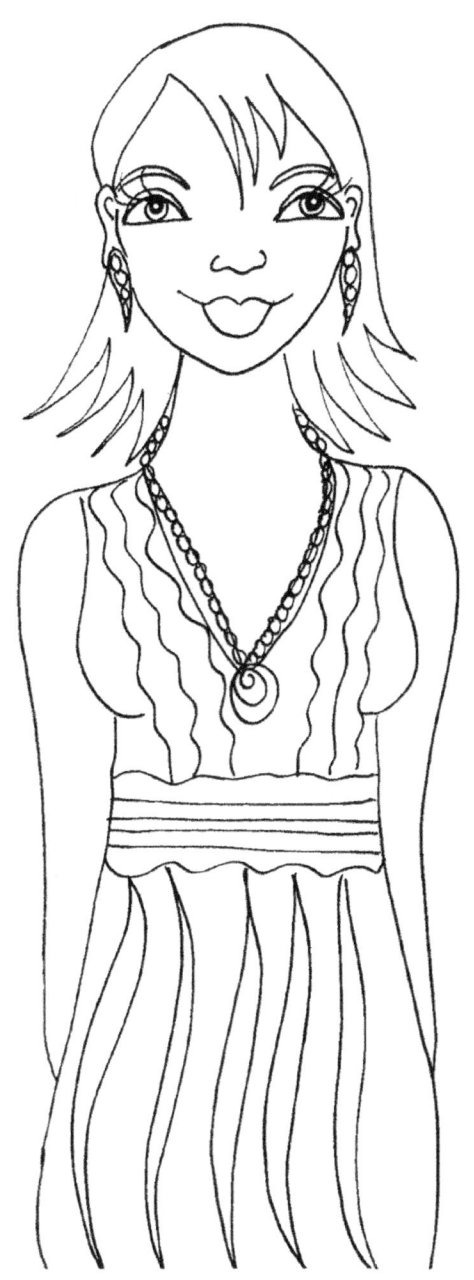

Be bold, be brave, be yourself

Pause
Breathe,
ask
your
inner
wisdom

7 | ABOUT JULIA HARVEY

Julia is originally from Liverpool, living in the Cotswolds with her Cornish Husband and two Jack Russells, one, a therapy dog and the other exceptionally cheeky.

She helps people calm their mind, soothe their soul and rebalance their life. Counsellor, Reiki Master, Artist, Author, Teacher with 25+ years experience, she has worked within therapeutic, educational and business settings. During this time, she has created an innovative holistic approach to finding balance born out of her own health crisis when she was in her 20s.

An Illustrator, Artist and Designer, Julia weaves all she knows and creates soothing soulful uplifting products and tools to bring a sense of calm and balance into people's daily lives. She works on private commissions, with corporate clients, heart centred business owners and stocks her shop with goodies.

Over the past 4 years, she has created The Muse Mantra Deck, Calendars, Diaries, Greeting Cards and now Muse Mantra Colouring Meditations.

She is also the author of two career coaching books and is currently writing, a guidebook called ReBalance Me, where she shares her 7 ways to wellness and her back to health journey.

www.juliaharveydesigns.co.uk
www.juliaharvey.co.uk

Printed in Great Britain
by Amazon